T0287864

PRAISE FOR
HURRICANES, LOVE AFFAIRS, & OTHER DISASTERS

In this collection of poems Susana Praver-Pérez bridges the
intimate relationships among culture, society and nature to
expose what is broken, damaged and diseased in our lives. But
her poems also reveal the healing and repair needed to become
whole in a fractured world. Forces of nature figure prominently
in her vibrant imagery but so do the everyday struggles of
people seeking refuge from exterior and interior—natural and
unnatural disasters. Her intense and poignant observations
are woven into a textured understanding of injustice, the social
and sexual body and the yearning for the restoration of human
dignity and tenderness.

NAOMI H. QUIÑONEZ
poet and PhD of Cultural Studies

MORE PRAISE

Heart wrenching and heart mending—from raised fist shout outs, to the mourning "wail of 4,000 dead," to the impotence of witness and the reverberation of trauma left in "Yemaya's blue wake" when "backs were turned and doors locked tight"—this collection unveils the contradictions of paradise, the disillusion of "streets of gold," the power plays between partners, and the exquisite agony of survival as *mujer*, as nation, as brave border crossers, *aquí y allá*, in "Borinquen" y "Afuera" recovering, designing, aligning – land, ocean, species – in response to injustice "unmasked, brought into full focus."

From the call of *boleros, plena, y bomba* to the response of Titi Sara's hips and *arroz con gandules*, Susana's *homenajes* are intimate and porous like a rainforest canopy, a soundtrack of dignity, vibrating with ancestral echoes, *recetas, y "herencias,"* painting a road map ever *pa'lante, como un elefante.*

These verses are tall stubborn ceiba trees, rooted, resistant, resilient, a refuge in full regalia adorned in defiance at the center of the tempest that colonialism, racism and patriarchy have whipped across the landscape for centuries. These love songs remind the reader that from the *escombros*, we dig out, we march, under the full moon "on a mission," with "sacred rage and indignant love," with "mother-prayers upon my lips," we rebuild with sass, with swing, with poetry.

Our collective beauty is our unity, our grace and guiding star, as we navigate a daily path elevating and amplifying our stories, *con sabrosura*, in the spirit and syncopated lyrics of the late great Ray Barreto, *de raíces aguadillanos, "Ay, unidos venceremos y yo sé que llegaremos, con sangre nueva, ¡indestructible!"*

SANDRA GARCÍA RIVERA

poet, musician,
host of Lunada Literary Lounge
& Open Mic, SF, 2010–2018

NOMADIC PRESS

OAKLAND

111 FAIRMONT AVENUE
OAKLAND, CA 94611

BROOKLYN

475 KENT AVENUE #302
BROOKLYN, NY 11249

WWW.NOMADICPRESS.ORG

MASTHEAD

FOUNDING AND MANAGING EDITOR
J. K. FOWLER

ASSOCIATE EDITOR
MICHAELA MULLIN

DESIGN
JEVOHN TYLER NEWSOME

MISSION STATEMENT

Through publications, events, and active community participation, Nomadic Press collectively weaves together platforms for intentionally marginalized voices to take their rightful place within the world of the written and spoken word. Through our limited means, we are simply attempting to help right the centuries' old violence and silencing that should never have occurred in the first place and build alliances and community partnerships with others who share a collective vision for a future far better than today.

INVITATIONS

Nomadic Press wholeheartedly accepts invitations to read your work during our open reading period every year. To learn more or to extend an invitation, please visit: www.nomadicpress.org/invitations

DISTRIBUTION

Orders by teachers, libraries, trade bookstores, or wholesalers:

Small Press Distribution
1341 Seventh Street
Berkeley, California 94701
spd@spdbooks.org
(510) 524-1668 / (800) 869-7553

Hurricanes, Love Affairs, & Other Disasters

This book was made possible by a loving community of chosen family and friends, old and new.

For author questions or to book a reading at your bookstore, university/school, or alternative establishment, please send an email to info@nomadicpress.org.

Cover artwork by Luís Pérez

Published by Nomadic Press, 111 Fairmount Avenue, Oakland, California 94611

First printing, 2021
Second printing, 2022

Library of Congress Cataloging-in-Publication Data

Title: *Hurricanes, Love Affairs, & Other Disasters*

p. cm.

Summary: *Hurricanes, Love Affairs, & Other Disasters* by Susana Praver-Pérez is a time capsule of the five-year period from 2016 to 2021, captured in poetry filled with mesmerizing cadence and powerful imagery. Upon opening, be prepared to witness the anguish brought by Hurricane María and the damage caused by colonialism, COVID-19, racism and other injustices. But within, you will also find the gifts of romantic and familial love and the tenderness of a grandmother's hands. This book weaves a wide range of subjects into a lyrical tapestry wrapped in hope.

[1. POETRY / General. 2. POETRY / Subjects & Themes / Places / Puerto Rico. 3. POETRY / Subjects & Themes / Colonialism. 4. POETRY / Women Authors. 5. POETRY / American / General.]

LIBRARY OF CONGRESS CONTROL NUMBER: 2020949245

ISBN 13: 978-1-955239-04-2

HURRICANES, LOVE AFFAIRS,
& OTHER DISASTERS

SUSANA PRAVER-PÉREZ

HURRICANES, LOVE AFFAIRS,
& OTHER DISASTERS

SUSANA PRAVER-PÉREZ

**NOMADIC
PRESS**

for
my parents
who gave me life
and
encouragement
to make good use of that
gift

&

para
la isla del encanto
y a todos aquellos
que
la aman
y
la defienden

contents

2. AFUERA

notes
classroom guide

foreword

A masterful storyteller, the poet Susana Praver-Pérez speaks of dreams and origins, of the lines of hands and maps woven together like the bodies that crossed the Atlantic from Africa into slavery, from Eastern Europe to Ellis Island, or those that were driven from Puerto Rico to New York City in the era of the great migrations. In a testimonial mode that honors the dead and uplifts the living, Susana creates new symbols and haunting images to depict this era of abandonment, this season of death and disease. "Black sandals" and shoeless cobblers, homeless men behind brown fences, and brown children crossing the desert alone, leap out at the reader, forcing us to respond, to position and situate ourselves in front of the catastrophes that we have witnessed, such as Covid-19, police killings of Black people, and the (re)colonization of the Caribbean and the Americas.

San Francisco, Los Angeles, Oakland, New York City, and Puerto Rico become the dramatic scenery of processes of displacement and dispossession, familiar scenarios of human and natural disasters, and bruised and runaway women—expected "refugees of a world on fire," as Cherrie Moraga once said. This is a world where "brown children with foreign tongues" and girls with black curly hair are made to feel like outsiders.

Susana, the artist, has a remarkable capacity to transform perception into epiphany, describe glimpses of immortality in poems of damage and desire where the "echoes of ancestors" run down the mean streets of history. Yet this is also a space for radical tenderness and the rebuilding of a new love. The love that runs through the pages of *Hurricanes, Love Affairs & Other Disasters* is not an ordinary one. It is at times an aching and tender mode of affection, a deep and curious gaze into "the science of pleasure," or a language of familial understanding where parents, grandparents, children, and other relatives are part of the connecting tissue of multiple diasporas and cultural lineages. These are poems that disarm the reader, leaving them "vulnerable/as a fetus/floating in its mama's womb."

Susana, the author, has a remarkable lyrical sensibility—usually accompanied by an unpredictable playfulness that spills over the page, intensifying reality—that has the ability to enter the consciousness of girls, teenagers, older women and men alike, with equal mastery. In a perpetual thought-provoking voice, she invites the readers and their imagination to "picture this," "decolonize your mind," to look into photographs of racial unbelonging, mistaken identities, and pillaged land, in her "querido Caribe."

The evocative power of Susan Praver-Pérez brings to life luminous moments of spiritual exaltation: "I don't remember my dreams / only the wine stains they leave." These are the instances when the reader is drawn into the aesthetic experience vibrant literature

provides, the mystical connection to ordinary and extraordinary events, reminding us that in the best poems, like those of this book, every experience is extraordinary.

VIOLETA OROZCO

Violeta Orozco is a bilingual writer from Mexico City, author of *The Broken Woman Diaries* and two other poetry collections. A translator at *Nueva York Poetry Review*, poet, and Ph.D. scholar of Chicanx and Latinx literature at University of Cincinnati, Orozco seeks to restore the fractured links between the broken bones and languages of the Americas.

introduction

On September 20, 2017, Puerto Rico became Hurricane María's bullseye. Brutal winds knocked out the island's infrastructure. Lacking food, potable water, gas and electricity, millions struggled day-to-day to stay alive.

Many lost the battle, some 3,000 by official estimates. (4,645 by the Harvard School of Medicine's estimates.) Among them was Sara Morales, my aunt by marriage, who died of sepsis in an ill-equipped San Juan hospital 41 days after the storm.

My relationship with Puerto Rico began in 1978 when I met the love of my life, a fiercely proud Boricua from Aguadilla. For decades, we lived with one foot here in the States and one on the island. When my husband passed away in 2007, I was left to tend the home fires both here and in Puerto Rico where my large, extended in-law family spreads from Aguadilla to San Juan. After the hurricane, the powerlessness to help or even reach them by phone to inquire about their well-being was painful.

When Titi Sara died, my frustration with the staggeringly slow relief effort by the U.S. government exploded in rage. The entire island and diaspora were erupting, indignant at the way Puerto

Rico has been exploited and mistreated as a colony. The anemic response to the hurricane was just the latest in a litany of affronts. What the winds left behind was colonialism unmasked, brought into full focus.

Puerto Rico flooded my thoughts, saturated my poetry and for a while, I could write about nothing else. But there is much in our world that shouts out for a poet's prism; requires translation into a language that distills lived truths from the headlines.

When children were separated from their parents at our southern border, anti-immigrant rhetoric rang harsh in my ears which bear witness to the struggles of my patients at La Clínica de la Raza. I listen as they speak of the encircling violence that drove them from their homes. I have heard so many heart-splitting stories; they sometimes permeate my dreams and enter my poems.

After finding physical safety and sustenance, connecting with others emotionally is a basic human motivator. I myself have entered romantic relationships trying to find that sense of "home" in a kindred spirit I knew before being widowed. I have yet to find a new "home" that is without cobwebs in the corners, skeletons in the closets or cracks in the windows through which winds howl. But at the very least, I have been inspired to write poems that celebrate connections and help put failed relationships behind me.

I combine break-up poems with others that decry colonialism because power dynamics between nations are often mirrored in

interpersonal relationships. When for example, domination is at work, its tools are similar whether the setting is an island nation floating in the Caribbean or one's own kitchen table.

We are living in a time of escalating disasters, both "natural" and societal. As a species, we have treated this lovely planet recklessly. Climate change is the consequence. Infernos that rage across huge swaths of forests and mega-storms that chew up islands in their path are unfortunately the "new normal."

But there are tender buds of fresh beginnings even amid the rubble of disasters. Precious connections and immeasurable acts of kindness occur within recovery as communities rebuild, and shared goals prove to be more important than perceived disunions. This is where hope lives.

And just like in the aftermath of a broken love affair that scatters bits of hearts on the ground, a stronger sense of self may emerge as we glue fragments back together.

SUSANA PRAVER-PÉREZ

Dazzled

Never has there been
a wind like this. Its throaty
howl has memorized
my name...
    ~Patricia Smith, *Blood Dazzler*
    (a collection of poems about
    Hurricane Katrina)

I am 37,000 feet above Des Moines,
  midway between New York City and San Francisco.
I am 1,200 miles north of New Orleans,
  midway through *Blood Dazzler*.

I turn off the overhead light so my travel companions cannot see
  the flood down my cheeks
  soaking cocktail napkins.

Once, I heard Patricia Smith speak
  of writing deep into painful themes.
One must, she said—
    someone in your audience needs it,
      is waiting for it,
    for reasons you may never know.

I didn't know I was waiting for it
　　　'til Ms. Smith's book broke me
　　　　　like a levee.

　　　　▬ ▬ ▬ ▬ ▬

I am 1,200 miles north of New Orleans
　　　where María's cousin Katrina stomped her feet,
　　　yelled obscenities
　　　　　of water and wind
　　　'til rooftops became life rafts.

I saw Katrina in photos,
　　　but I smelled María's fetid breath,
　　　saw how she left Borinquen
　　　　　black in the night sky,
　　　a massif of wreck,
　　　muted as a boneyard.

Weeks of dead dial tones
　　　and error beeps before voices
　　　emerged from the miasma.
Tití's voice—soaked by storm,
　　　a garbled cry for help
　　　　　too late.

I write into the ache María left behind.

　　　　▬ ▬ ▬ ▬ ▬

I am 37,000 feet above Des Moines
    remembering when
    my son left home for Iowa,
        running from our fractured lives.

    The wounds left by what bruised us
        still ache.

I lean into that ache,
    craving healing,
    waiting to celebrate
        wide aloud.

Maybe I'm too loud,
    the way I talk in dancehall tones—

    He speaks softly, defies
        my fading ears.
    He is home again,
        but sometimes silence
        drapes like gossamer
            between us.

I write into the silence,
    lift that moist gauze,
    clean air soothing wounds.

I am 37,000 feet above Des Moines,
        1,200 miles north of New Orleans.
I am open wide
        as the centerspread, spine
        pressed against leatherette, hurtling
        through the air faster
                than a hurricane.

Someone once said of my dizzying speed,
        What you are running from
        must have fearsome teeth.

        I claimed to be running
                not from, but to,
        didn't see the damage
                denial can do
        'til I saw the slash
                my eye-tooth left—
        razor in an armored smile.

                ━ ━ ━ ━ ━

I sit solemn in a straight-back chair,
        bare feet dusting earth.
There is nowhere else to run.
The quiet in the air is no longer silence,
        but listening.

I write in that stillness,
tears turned to blue ink,
    salvaged seeds of new beginnings
        moist and mine
            in my palms.

1.
BORINQUEN

Commentary on the $72 Billion Debt: A Short History of Puerto Rico

Your beauty was
      your downfall.
Men with beards and arms,
      enamored by your riches,
Wanted you
      for themselves.
Slew Tainos suckling at your breast.
Swapped brown bodies
      with black ones
      ripped from Yoruba lands.
Spewed seed
      across your fertile belly.
Raised cane
      and mulatos.

More men came
      with blue eyes and legalese
      protesting your rape.
In your relief you fell
      for tricks.

They pimped you piously, got rich
        as you scavenged for scraps,
        begged for *habichuelas*,
While they hawked you
        to the highest bidder.

And as you stand there,
        beautiful cheeks sunken with hunger,
        skirts dirty and shredded
        like palm fronds,
They dare to tell you,
        It's your own damn fault.

Querido Caribe (Spanish)

No dejo de pensar en ti.

La luz se apagó
en el archipiélago.

Los que se creen tus dueños
te barren
como si fueras escombros.
Pretenden no conocer tu nombre
ni el robo de las riquezas
de tus montañas,
tus bosques,
y el sudor de tu frente.

Las bocas secas, los cuerpos sudados
anhelan agua dulce.
La ayuda proviene de aquellos
que no tienen nada
compartiendo
su olla de arroz.

Y a pesar de bloqueos y fronteras belicosas,
un artista, desde la Plaza de la Revolución,
pinta un gallo gigante,
un Caballo de Troya,
lleno de amor.
Esa es su arma
en esta guerra de guerrillas.

Siempre,
La Victoria

Querido Caribe (English)

I can't stop thinking of you.

The light has gone out
      across the archipelago.

Those who think they own you
      brush you away
      like debris,
Claim to not know your name
or the profits pillaged
      from your mountains,
      your cane fields,
      the sweat of your brow.

Parched mouths, sweltering bodies
      crave sweet water.
Help comes from those with bare shelves
      sharing their pot of rice.

And despite blockades and bellicose borders,
an artist, in his Plaza de la Revolución garret,
      paints a giant *gallo*,
      a Trojan Horse
      filled with love.
That is his weapon
      in this guerilla war.

Siempre,
La Victoria

María

It was the winds ~
        terror winds
        signed in as Sacred Mother
        to fool the faithful.

Not just winds ~ monster gales
        twisting towers with bare hands,
        turning battens meant to protect
        into projectiles.

It had to be the wind that turned
        the line that divides the living from the dead
        into crêpe paper ribbons
        spiraling high overhead.

That brutal wind raged so hard
        Boricuas spinning in the air didn't know
        on which side of the line
        they would land.

When the winds calmed, we in the diaspora dropped pebbles
        in rising waters, but there were no ripples.
        We strained to hear through throbbing silence,
        but not even the *coquís* sang.

Querida Isla, ¿Estás allí? Háblame por favor—Qué me contesta—Algo,
Algo por favor—¡por favor!

We gathered to wait, holding one another
  even if we didn't know
  each other's names.
Drums pounding like heart beats broke the silence.
Bomba dancers in prayerful trance whirled skirts in María's wake.
A crescendo of voices and maracas sounded fervent pleas...

  ...and then I saw you across the room.

It must have been the wind and that broken border
  between the breathing and the dead
  that brought you back though your ashes swirl
  above Aguadilla ten years now.

Elegant in a white *guayabera,* a soft wind caressed
  your thick black hair. I longed to touch
  your sepia skin as I watched your hands
  make the *cueros* sing.

Sweet reminiscence, we rambled amid calm winds
  in Santurce, Utuado, Piñones, Arecibo, El Yunque, Corozal,
  till you told of the tempest that shattered these places,
  red earth flowing like blood.

I asked who the winds had taken.
  Your dark eyes brightened ~

our family had survived,
hands held high amid fallen palms.

I whispered prayers on autumn winds, but you disappeared
like ocean mist. My tears fell in waves of loss ~
some fresh, some timeworn, some still unfolding
as the *barriles* played a mournful *cuembe*.

After the Storm: A Sonata in the Key of C Minor

In growing shade of fractured walls
A man lilts a mournful solo lute
Downcast by the scale of ruin
He sees his island's life unroofed

Vultures hiss in dark gray skies
Raindrops clang on walls of tin
A timpani plays a promenade
Rat-tat-tats disordered din

A desolate poet begins to chant
A saxophone wails in soulful pain
A subdued hush on distant strings
A lantern flickers through twisted cane

Pictures drift on waning winds
Cry, a deep bass, sad ascent
Breathless, anxious, leaping high
A fight to flee stiff confines

A bell is struck with enormous force
A procession slogs at slowing speed
English horns creep as fury mounts
Lunges, trembles, lands in a heap

Hunger swarms in chaotic bazaars
As infrastructure's shape dissolves
Sorrow thrums a low brass hum
An endless requiem as loss evolves

Picture This

She picks through rubble
    of her storm-ripped home,
        a spring dribbles
            down a rocky hill,
                red clay oozes
                    between bare toes.
She gathers water
    in a soda bottle,
        shirt splashed
            with the words:
                Enjoy Every Moment.

Who captured her photo,
    feet sunk *fango* deep
        in Utuado?

Who saw her reach for help
    and receive
  a bag of Cheez-Its and a FEMA form
    to be filed online
        on an island without power?

Will *Life Magazine* follow
    this abandoned Boricua?
      Know if she fell ill

to leptospirosis
        spawned in rat-pissed rivers?
If scabies burrowed her sun-cracked skin
        with no medicine for the maddening itch?

Will they inquire how long
        water and light lay stagnant
                in her island's fractured veins?

Will she join the thirsty throngs
        swamping Luís Muñoz-Marín
                International Airport?

Hundreds of thousands,
        a suitcase and a one-way ticket in hand,
                exploding
        into the diaspora
                like a geyser of pure water
                she only prays she had.

Poeta en San Juan

This is not hell, but the street.
       ~Federico García Lorca, *Poeta en Nueva York*

aquí, en las calles de esta ciudad, they pray
their tropical dreams will come true again.
       ~Barbara Jane Reyes, *Poeta en San Francisco*

Aquí, on San Juan's tangled streets,
clouds of bees reclaim honey
       sipped from tasseled cane,
       bent like stolen souls
       in broken *cañaverales*.

Amid mounds of debris,
billows of bees search out sugar
       in cast-off cans of *Coco Rico*
       and *BoriCola, zafra de azúcar*
       in urban *zafacones*.

Don't kill the bees! they said.
Spread the word from mouth to ear,
       hand to skin, pulse of *Plena*—
       hand to mouth, mouth to ear,
       Don't kill the bees!

Bees' breath on broken flowers
Will return mango and plantain
      to storm stripped slopes,
      will pollinate recovery,
      germinate a future.

Mosquitos feast on human blood
As people sleep
      on rooftops,
      escaping
      hot molasses nights.

But bees live on nectar, sweet as *boleros*
Sung in the light of a blue moon,
      hum love songs to the earth,
      caress velvet petals,
      drink *almíbar* at noon.

In blossoms' stark absence,
Someone set out sugar water
      on sidewalks
      for bees circling
      in an arc.

Save the bees! they said.
Spread the word from mouth to ear,
      hand to skin, pulse of *Plena*—
      hand to mouth, mouth to ear,
      ¡Bendito!—the bees will save us.

Ode to Tití

Tití Sara could squeeze juice from a dime.
And when she ran out of dimes,
Tití could suck sap from a *centavo*.

They say oil and water don't mix,
        but Tití knew how
to water *aceite vegetal*, make it last
        'til her next paycheck.

Tití opened her triple-locked door,
        embraced me
        in her freckled arms—
        Aquí tienes tu casa. Siempre.

As soon as I settled,
I skipped to the market—
        café y queso,
        piña y parcha,
      slipped fine Spanish olive oil
        into my cart,
            succulent frill
            for her cupboard.

¡¡Por qué compraste tanto!? she quizzed
        as I hauled in the shopping,

voice the tone of her short copper hair.

You're gonna eat all that? she asked.
We're gonna eat all that! I replied,
    storing the rice with a wink
      of my eye.

Tití cooked *arroz con gandules,*
    plátanos fritos,
    pechuga de pollo
      steeped in *sofrito.*

No sooner than plates were laid on the table,
    we heard a *tok-tok-tok!* at the door.

    ¡Buen día Sarita!

Olga from down the hall,
    in house dress and shawl,
    to borrow some olive oil,
    ¡Si me haces el favor!

¡Cierto! said Sara, jumped like an athlete,
    poured half her flask of oil in a jar.
¡Toma! she said, with the grace of a dancer.

    Así fue Tití.

If Tití had two dollars, she'd give one
　　　to a *tecato* trembling on the corner,
　　　spend days and nights aiding the ill.

But where was the aid when Tití got ill? After María
　　　knocked out electric, left her
　　　sin agua, eating canned tuna
　　　'til her intestines jammed.

Where was the aid? Stuck in her building,
　　　car soaked to chassis in hurricane surge.

Pallets of water left on a runway,
　　　　　while Tití and thousands withered
　　　　　　　　with thirst.
Tití died
　　　　　en el Hospital del Maestro,
　　　　surgery soiled by darkness and heat.

Dancing barefoot with angels *al camposanto,*

　　　Así fue Tití.

The shoes she left, too huge to fill,
　　　stand empty—
　　　　　　　frente al Capitolio
　　　　　and the White House lawn,
　　　　　　　silent witness
　　　　to what went so wrong.

How to Keep Cool When a Hurricane Knocks Out the Power

Do not call up wind—you already know
the great god *Huracán* who spewed
his bitter breath on you. Do not speak his words—
they have already burned your mouth,
tumbled your walls, beheaded your palm trees.

> Do call up breeze, that delicate air
> found on wings of *colibris* and seafoam,
> scent of *salitre* a trail of perfume
> in Yemaya's blue wake.

Do not call up snow—that blanket of whiteness
Tío Joe sent photos of from Nueva York seeking
the sustenance those from the north made
so hard to find, fields of *viandas* buried
beneath concrete and debt.

> Do call upon the white sparkle of rain
> that doubles as drink and nurtures veiled roots.
> Boil *yucca y lluvia* 'til your *abuela* appears in the vapor,
> *agua de coco* cupped in her wrinkled hands.

Do not give up as you stand in line
five hours to buy gasoline for generators
that poison your lungs and fill your ears
with shrill, like the wail of 4,000 dead,
decomposing in the tropical sun.

Do hang a hammock on a rooftop
where you can see
the moon and stars and remember
the great god *Huracán*
was your great-great-great-grandfather,
and your bones are carved of ironwood,
your blood a braid of many mothers,
espíritu long and strong as *el Río Grande de Loíza*.

Yes, one day, there will be cool *jugo de parcha* to sip again,
because resilience will always be your middle name.

Return: Against the Flow

An old man with hair dyed black
       like in better days,
              flashes a toothless smile.

He is so proud of his little house for sale,
shows me the cramped *cocina* and soot-filled *sala*
       all built with his very own hands.

The children he raised have all gone.
       He sits on his porch alone
              watching Puerto Rico pivot
                     on the point of a pin.

Where will you go? I ask.
¡Afuera! he spouts, Away!

I have come to find a home
       of my own,
sink deep in this island
       that feeds my soul.

I am a car in the bus lane
driving against the flow
       on a one-way street.

People wave wild arms
        to stop me.

Nena, ¡! Qué tú haces!? ... What are you doing!?

They can't fathom why
I'd plant feet on cratered streets,
        entangle myself
        in an unraveling realm.

Their worries and warnings
        cleave my dreams,
        leave me questioning.

I see fresh green sprouting
        through cracked concrete.

                They show me old green mold
                        invading houses.

I see red stripes and a single star shimmering
        in an aqua sky.

                They show me red blood
                        of a nation crushed by promises.

Landscapes shift with every turn.

A hilltop mansion bathed in gold

looks down on a sea of blue
FEMA tarps
still topping fractured houses
two years after the storm.

My mind is a cyclone of queries:

How many chickens can run free
on urban streets
and still call it city?
How many feral cats can fit
in a vacant house?
How many abandoned pups can roam
beaches and backroads
before the call of the wild turns
all to dog eat dog?

How can I tell if the sun piercing
the mangroves is sunrise
or sunset?

I pray for answers, I pray for Puerto Rico.

A wrinkled *viejita* in a well-ironed housedress
rocks on her porch as I pass,
wishes me *un buen día,*
blesses me with her heartfelt *bendición*
while *Preciosa* plays softly
in the background.

Better Homes & Gardens: Puerto Rico Edition, January 2019

Ramón had a way with women and words,
introduced me to Lucecita at the corner café.

Mi amiga, he named me, though we'd barely met.
Lucecita Benítez! Her name sparked

vinyl memories, eardrums and soul.
Does she still sing? I whispered a bit too loud.

The diva's brow turned angry sea, turned
category three hurricane he quickly calmed.

We returned to our coffee, shared
stories from *niñez* 'til now.

He painted pictures in the air,
the grand home of his youth,

a splash of roses in the garden
his mother loved to tend.

We spoke of Spain—if he ever left,
that's the place he'd go.

Not stateside, with its Coca-Cola culture
and biased, blinkered eyes. *Pero, na'*—

he wasn't going anywhere—just counting
blessings, like stars mirrored on the sea.

We both loved houses, mourned
the ones ripped wide by brutal winds.

I laid bare my pockets,
shared my front-porch dreams.

Eye to eye, he vowed to find me
my garden of roses, my roof of *flamboyán*.

We wandered San Juan streets, the back-story of each
shattered house or empty lot like gossip across a fence:

> *Mira*, that full square block in front of SuperMax? Bought
> by an investor. *¡Todo! Imagínate los millones y las palas* in their pockets.

> And that graffitied row on *Calle del Parque? ¡Coño!* They offered
> *un montón,* but she won't sell to vultures flying circles in the sky.

We walked a while in silence, shook our heads,
watched history unfurl like a lopsided prizefight.

30

My needs are simple, I said—a bath, a bed,
a place to cook, close to my family and friends.

I'm not afraid to rescue
salt-stained walls, polish rusted rails.

Como esa—I pointed to a rundown house
caked with cats, choked with vines.

Ramón had a way with women and words,
clacked the neighbor's door like a *clave*.

¡Buen día Señora! he sang, lauding her garden
and luck—the winds had spared her wooden house.

Her wizened face became that of a girl, opening
her barred door a little wider.

And the house next door? he asked. *Ay, mijo,* she sighed,
shaking her white-curled head. *Pues, tú sabes...La herencia...*

We sang the chorus in harmony, *Ay, yay, yay!! La herencia...*
dead-end sinking us like a tsunami.

The laws of inheritance, penned to protect,
orphaned the house, legal title stuttering in the air.

Tú sabes, said the *señora.*
Tú sabes...y así, the stories begin.

Water View House for Sale

Why would they put a desk on an outdoor deck? I ask
      browsing photos of a house
         in Humacao

I flip through pics and answers dawn

Not a deck ~ this was once a room
      before María ripped the roof off
         this family's home

I scroll through
      leaf-littered living room
      water-logged cabinets
      paint-blistered walls

FEMA never arrived
Light arrived late
They locked the gate and left

Who pays a mortgage for an uninhabitable house?
Who can pay when jobs are shuttered
      and salaries shrink?

Banks licked lips
        like *El Lobo*
        in the Three Little Pigs
                huffing and puffing
                as walls blew down

No matter the house was made of brick
        housed three generations
        bodas and births
        vidas y velorios

Too many *velorios*
        for uncounted dead
Backyard burials
        as water rose

                to chest

                        to chin

                                to top of head

        Underwater

This house is underwater
This house is lot #366 on Auction.com
        is a Handyman's Special
        an Investor's Delight
        a Vulture's Feast

Underwater

This nation is underwater
This nation is drowning in *corruptos'* debt
        is a roll of bills in a rich man's pocket
        is coming up for air on cobblestone streets
        is learning to swim ~
                raised arms parting water

Castles in the Air

You could walk right by,
      not even see the lime-colored house
      amid thick emerald leaves.

Or its owner—*señora* of seventy years—
      her rocker in rhyme with a song of *coquís.*

Yellow-bloomed vines tangle grills on windows.
Mango tree shadows a battered tin roof—
      just a blue FEMA tarp
      between her and the rain.

Far worse, her sister's house next door—
      its roof torn wide by María's shrill wind.

Rain runs down walls blackened with mold.
Rust gnaws at a filigreed gate.

All her years as a lawyer are crumbling—
      she's perched like a bird,
      her front porch, her cage.

Pensions dissolve in fiscal default
      on an island held hostage
         by foreign dictates.

But this is her home,
    her haven,
    her castle,
jasmín y sofrito perfume the air.

New moon nights were splendored with stars
    before bright light
    high-rise buildings appeared.

Flamboyán y flores were felled to roll asphalt,
    parking lots spread to the edge of her green.

And now they want to bulldoze her house,
    demolish its walls and her dreams.

But each new day, aroma of coffee,
    radio playing an old *le lo lai,*
she keeps the beat, the creak of her rocker
    repeating...repeating,
    a defiant reply.

Cleaning House
(reflections on the ouster of
Governor Ricardo Roselló)

I'm tossing useless *I Love You*'s—
    a polyester rose,
    a heart-shaped balloon.
    I have no room
        for words without feet,
        for one-way streets.

I'm tired of insults—
    puta, pata, pendeja,
    crush them
        in my upraised fist.

I'm tearing sheets—
    tying them to balconies,
    dangling in the air,
    a single star
        between my teeth.

I'm trashing the commonwealth—
    there is no common wealth
    when you loot and leave
        bare shelves.

I'm taking my seat at the table—
      been fed scraps
      in the pantry
         too long.

I'm standing tall —
      an ocean of Boricuas
        rising.

¡Coño! ¡Qué bello amanecer!

Cartography
of the Caribbean

Once, during "the discovery,"
mapmakers placed Borinquen
      at the center
      of the New World.
North America, not fully explored,
         was mapped like a snake dangling above
         the island renamed Puerto Rico
         for riches the Spaniards found.

The snake grew voracious teeth.
Gold was devoured.
   Ore became sugarcane
      then petrol
         pharmaceuticals
            a tax haven
               a post-hurricane clearance sale
                  Se Vende signs seen everywhere.

So, it sounds like old news when geologists explain
shake after shake of earthquake swarms:

      The North American plate is pushing hard
      against the Caribbean, *apretando*

'til fault lines jolt,
rocks explode,
and Boricuas with frayed, singed nerves
feel they're about to implode.

Houses built on pillared legs
fall to their knees.
Schools collapse
like tents of cards.
Thousands of people sleep under the stars, afraid
they'll be crushed by their homes.

And every blackout chafes
half-healed wounds
remembering
a year without light,
months without water,
weeks of waking to tell your daughter
Eat your rice, *mi amor* ~
No hay nada más.

Cascades of disasters reshape
inner landscapes
like swarms of quakes reshape
Puerto Rico's topography.

In just fifteen days, the city of Ponce sunk
fifteen feet, slid westward towards the setting sun.

On *Día de los Reyes,* Guayanilla woke
    to find *Punta Ventana* shattered ~
        porthole in the stony cliff
        now jagged row of teeth.

And in Guánica, point of entry when the U.S. invaded in 1898,
    the ocean trembles.

On the shore, a woman watches
    a meteor streak across the sky.
Her house is a mound of rubble
    but she's still standing
        listening to the *coquís*
            singing in the mangroves.

2.
AFUERA

Unaccompanied Minors: For Those Who Have Forgotten

No one leaves home unless
home is the mouth of a shark...
home is the barrel of the gun
~ Warsan Shire

Streets of gold glistened in imaginations
    across blood-stained villages.
They could nearly see the skirts
    of a verdigris woman perched in the harbor
        welcoming them
    as they cowered among chickens and mules
        waiting
    for Cossacks' attacks
        to pass,
    for brutal wars and drug lords
        to pass.

Home had become the barrel of a gun.

1.
Grandma Sarah was twelve years old
    when she crossed the Atlantic.

Alone.
There was no time to wait
        as shtetls burned in blazing hate.

Her mother
        hugged her tight to her breast,
        braided her thick brown hair,
        wrapped her in a woolen shawl,
        pinned a cousin's name in her pocket.

Harsh seas and queries at Ellis Island were her border crossing.

Grandma Sarah spoke no English when she arrived.
There was no gold to dazzle her
        young eyes
And Lady Liberty's skirts were stiff and cold to touch.
Not like the fabric her small hands were tasked to turn
        into shirts and suits
                in Lower East Side sweatshops.

Any silver that crossed her palm was sent
        to bring parents and siblings
                to this strange land
        where families breathed stale air
                in tuberculous tenements.

They were the lucky ones,
Gaining entry under America's disdainful eye
        before the gates slammed shut

and refugees were turned away
while smoke and ash of brethren's bodies rose to the sky
in Auschwitz, Treblinka, Sobibór...

Backs were turned and doors locked tight.

Quotas had been met, it was explained,
and they were children
with dirty faces
and foreign tongues.

2.

Graciela Sánchez was twelve years old
when she crossed the desert.
Alone.
There was no time to wait for permits or visas
as her brothers' bullet-riddled bodies
lay bathed in blood
in the front room of her family's home.

Her mother
hugged her tight to her breast
shaved her long black hair
dressed her in boy's garb
blessed her with the sign of the cross.

Parched days and ice-cold nights were her border crossing.

Graciela Sánchez spoke no English when she arrived.

There was no gold to dazzle her
        young eyes
And Lady Liberty's skirts were stiff and cold to touch.
Not like the fruits and flowers her small hands were
        tasked to sell on street corners
                in Oakland, San Francisco, Los Angeles...

Any silver that crossed her palm was sent
        to bring parents and siblings
                to this strange land
        where *familias* breathed foul air
                in crowded apartments.

They were the lucky ones,
Crossing a jagged border under America's disdainful eye
        without being captured, incarcerated, left in legal limbo
        while brethren's bodies litter rocky fields
                in Guatemala, Honduras, El Salvador...

Backs were turned and doors locked tight.

There are waiting lists and legal channels, they explain,
        and after all, they add in hushed tones,
                they are brown children
                with dirty faces
                and foreign tongues.

Song of Refuge

If my song could hold tangled weeds of memory,
I would sing my grandmother's hands braiding bread
in a tense that is both then and now.

If the cracks through which we travel could channel my song,
I would sing echoes of beginnings
trailing like breadcrumbs.

My tousled tongue, etched with a new language,
struggles to recall words it once caressed
and the meaning of home changes with each passing year.

I have built a house with turquoise doors
open to all who hunger.
Now floorboards crumble beneath my feet.

If I am sent to wander once again,
my song will howl
like a dog, cold in the rain.

But if you, still sleeping, reach for me
with skin as warm as fresh baked bread,
shelter would blossom like a grandma's embrace.

Persimmon

Teresita taught me how to eat
persimmon, to crunch
the firm flesh of flattened spheres.

I am not from here. Did not know
fruits that float above bungalow roofs,
fall at your feet on evening walks
scented with jasmine and rose.

Did not know kumquat,
loquat, lychee—nor feijoa
feigning pineapple as the ripe fruit bursts
in my mouth. The tastes of Eden,
I think, coming from concrete cities
and seasons of snow.

Turning the corner of unknown streets,
my first glimpse of persimmon—
orange hearts in twilight sun,
leafless tree in fall's gray sky.

Back home we had quince, autumn fruit
of a knobby tree I loved to climb,
loved to fly on the wooden swing

that my father hung
from its dappled limbs.

Quince. Gnarled yellow pear,
so tart when raw it could twist
your lips inside out.

Our kitchen steamed aromas
acerbic and sweet
as my grandmother's hands
sliced and stewed, sugared and sieved,
whipped the stiff fruit,
purée for our table, silky and sweet
as ripe persimmon.

Something from Nothing
(eulogy for an uncle)

We played in the shade of his newspaper palms—
Pied piper with a harmonica,
     handkerchief mice leapt
     under three generations
     of squealing fingers.

We were captured in the magic web he spun
as he traveled 'round the sun a hundred times.

Now he climbs a paper ladder to the moon
crooning a farewell song
     in a dozen different tongues
     in which he learned
     to say goodbye.

Nightmares

I don't remember
my dreams, only the wine
    stains they leave
    on the nightstand,
how they make me feel
wary, like fists flung from shadows,
or the way love's underbelly sometimes snakes
    through broken glass.

We never heard "inherited trauma"
    growing up
but we absorbed it through our skin and the stories
    our grandmas whispered in Yiddish
    while they sipped tea
    through sugar cubes
        clenched between their teeth.

How could we believe there were no monsters
    in the closet
when we saw the navy-blue numbers
    tattooed on the cook's pale arm
        as he poured coffee
        at the station,
    heart pounding
        when a train rattled past?

The war that marked our parents' generation was over,
but how could we believe the world was safe at last
        while we ducked under desks
        in air raid drills?

        When we saw fanged dogs
        and high-pressure hoses
        turned on Black marchers
                on our Black & White TVs?

        When we heard Lady Day sing—
                black bodies swinging in the southern breeze
                strange fruit hanging from the poplar trees...

Half a century later not much has changed, except
        lynchings are now by bullet or knee
        and the drills in dark classrooms
        are for killers from within.

How can we tell children that monsters don't exist
        when they see their footprints in the mud?

Mistaken Identity: Facebook Pegged Me Wrong

I am not a "Mother of a Black Son"
    though Africa hums beneath the shield
    of my son's light skin, lineage
    inked as accents on his name.

I am not the mother of a Black son
but my son's *amigo de corazón*
    is dark like sweet *cacao*.

Borinquen beats more softly
in his than in my son's veins,
    but their roots aligned
        in Iowa.

Both were running from and to—
    One from Oakland where dried leaves crunched
        beneath his feet, death an echo in his ears.
    The other from Harlem where rose petals
        of his heart risked trample.

Growing tomato and basil, tending sheep, learning history
in Quaker community, they collected the pure quiet
        voice within.

Diplomas in hand, they left to university
        to prepare for a world that's tough
            on black and brown.

Four years later, cap and gown and a car
        packed with books, they journeyed
            past Spanish moss and Confederate flags.

 I held my breath
        'til they were safe
        in Harlem, my son like a nephew
            in his best friend's home.

Each now finds open arms
        on either coast, a last-minute call
            enough to reorder the day.

My mother-heart leapt, my son's best friend at my table,
        my house filled with laughter
            as we shared
        spiced dishes and dreams.

I am not the mother of this Black son
        but my mother-heart trembled
            as the dialog turned—
        ice down my spine as he told me—
            cold steel around bare wrists
            the slam of a cell door

the sparrow caged
            for near nothing.

I pushed away thoughts of Tamir Rice and Freddie Gray—
Could not make room for those heartbreaks
            in the same breath.

He dismissed danger, said he couldn't let his wings
            be clipped and still
                        fly.

            Sugar, I am not asking you be any less
                        than who you are,
            but Black Lives Matter
            means nothing to the mofos
                        with badges and guns.

I am not the mother of this Black son
            but we sat in the glow of a stained-glass lamp,
            mother-prayers upon my lips:

            I know you must soar—but know the bird,
                        glorious in flight,
                        is eyed with envy and fear—
            Keep your glinting wings
                        far from hunters' aim.

            I know you cannot promise safety,
                        but at least promise to remember

how loved you are,
how your footsteps help make the sun rise
each morning.

Sancocho

My son has a name a full hand of fingers long.
When the DMV made him fan all his names
        on a table, like a gin-rummy flush,
            he asked,
What were you and Pa thinking!?

What we were thinking was
        to paint the map of your being
            in such bright letters
        you would never lose yourself,
            never lose us,
        nor your grandparents, *tus abuelos*,
        your great-grandparents, *tus bisabuelos*,
            as you walk in a world
        where accent marks are seen as rubble
            to stumble on,
        and the roll of an "r" an aberration.

We stamped you with the world of my ancestors,
        or what we knew of it—
        after a genocidal war
        destroyed the shtetls of Europe
        and yanked those roots from the soil.

We gave you my paternal name
    which may not really be
    my father's name
    or my father's father's name,
        but a name
    a clerk at Ellis Island approximated;
    a name that in Russian may have been
    Pravda—meaning Truth.

The truth is hidden in an uprooted name.
We hold on tight to our names, always
seeking the truth.

Y tu Papá stamped his name and his roots
    on you, and on me too, embossed
    an ever-present Pérez
        on birth certificates,
        marriage licenses,
    and as you well know, *mijo,*
        drivers' licenses.

Pérez is like Smith in the Spanish-speaking world,
    but here, instead of the beautiful
        cascade of syllables it is,
    PÉ-rez is puréed into per-EZ
        by English-speaking mouths.

Never let them tell you how
to say your own name—

It is yours.

It is yours, and Papi's, and now mine.
It belonged to *abuelo* Mateo who lived
      in a wooden house with no hot water in Moca.
Y tu bisabuelo who walked those fertile hills barefoot,
      cracked soles caked with red soil.
Y tus tatara abuelos whose names were scrawled
      on the front page of a Bible, with a pencil
         sharpened by a machete.

Your roots spread deep and far
      in a land whose sweetness
      was sucked by *cañaverales*
      and colonizers.
Roots spreading
      like woody lianas
      and flowering vines
      in El Yunque.
Roots that spread
      through the halls of our home,
      shape glistening sulci in our brains,
      thickly seasoned braid of blood
         beating like *bomba* drums,
         strumming like a balalaika,
            spreading like verbs
            in our veins.

Behind the Eight Ball

Six in the corner pocket,
Sink seven in the side.
I was on a roll when they tried
To chase us out.

Click, clack, cue 'cross my back,
Pool hall nights, we don't want no fights.
We're still playing,
You know what I'm saying?

They called us "spics"—

I'd expect that in Queens
Where we threw barbs at each other
Like gray snowballs
From the gutter.

But not in Vermont
Where snow glistened
Like diamonds
In a white expanse.

In Queens, we knew how to flex
Our muscles no further
Than the next guy's line
In the sand.

But in this cold town,
Heads were hot—
Licked lips
Craved blood.

We could smell bourbon
On their breath
As frenzied fists
Found our jaws.

We called the cops
To save us,
But it was us they cuffed
For the "crime" of being brown.

Back in New York,
We took our beef to Lady Liberty.
Wondered about those promises
She'd whispered in our parents' ears.

Pigeonholes
(or, Toys-Are-Us)

We learned our place
        cooking cakes
                in pink plastic
                ovens
                toys made to persuade
                us girls
        how pleasant it is
        to wash and serve
                clean and bake

A bit like Tom Sawyer
        tricking passersby
        to paint a peeling fence
                as if they'd won
                first prize

Indoctrination in a box
    like the mini brooms and mops
    wrapped in images
        of brown girls and boys
        playing with these toys

On a nearby shelf
    pictures of a blond-haired boy
    embellish a toy chemistry set

Roles are bestowed
                early
    before the sun of all-equal-in-the-eyes-of-God
    rises

What Makes a Four Year Old Think She's Too Brown and Curly?

A fading photo lets me know
I am not imagining
the dark tango of curls
twirling on my head,
my olive skin,
white cotton dress,
green and red flowers blooming
on the bodice and hem,
skirt puffed like a parachute
floating me
into the unfamiliar—
my uncle's new house, perfumed
with new money, climbing
into America's lap.

Why does this not feel like family?
A Cadillac in the driveway,
cedar scent of cigar smoke,
grown-ups with something-or-other-
on-the-rocks, the pigs-in-a-blanket
skewered with toothpicks.

My cousin's soft blond
hair flosses her lace collar.
Her cousin, also flaxen,
is not my cousin—
they are quick to let me know.

Decades past a war where
pale and blond were camouflage
and brown a bullseye,
colorism still laps our shores
and class conflict
claims hostages.

In the photo, my arms are stiff,
anchored at my sides,
uncomfortable, like an outsider
looking in.

I want to coax the 4-year-old I was
to melt the steel in her shoulders,
raise her bronzed arms,
lift her voice in song, sing
to these seeming strangers—

I belong! I belong!

No, I'm Not the Maid, and Other Micro-Aggressions

Like water off a duck's back, they say.
But it isn't really.
A seed of contempt is planted
        as they gesture
                with dismissive fingers,
        speak with their backs,
        say "Puerto Rican"
                with a curled lip.

I read between the lines and attitude
        slides off the page,
                rattles like a tremor
                        shifting landscapes.

A whirling hiss of disdain
        becomes a tornado,
        knocks me
                off my feet
        before I even realize
                it's time to run for shelter.

Decolonize Your Mind

This is for the girls who run away,
  run so far to forget
  who they are.
Dive deep into suburbs of Any City, USA
Where no one knows
The why or the way
  a "D" disappears
  between vowels,
Or how "L" and "R" switch it up
In partner-dance twirls
  of the tongue.

This is for the *nenas* who move away
  to marry
Men with names like Smith and Jones
  to merge and blend,
Submerge and send *Que pasa* power
  to the closet
  with the well-ironed sheets
  stiff with *almidón*
  like *abuela* taught them
  before they left home.

This is for the *chicas*
Who scorch their scalps

with lye and flat irons,
Pressed by the myth
of *pelo malo.*
Who swallow so many
Barely masked slights
they sweat it
through their pores.

Who believe the lie
that they are less,
Not knowing their own magnificence.

Bendecida

He took what wasn't his
        sin permiso
Left his ancestors' echoes
        sin querer
Fed her bitter potions
        sin vergüenza
But mother love fiercely held on tight

With growing womb, he left her
        sin un quinto
She cursed his fading shadow
        sin tapujos
Embraced the budding life within
        sin pena
Surged with awe when child revealed her might

She had no words for this blessing
        sin parejo
Held baby girl and brought her home
        sin nombre
A month of days slid by
        sin darse cuenta
Before she found a name she knew was right

A name fluttered in the autumn air
sin dudas
In a language not her own
sin inquietar
She named this blessed being
sin apuros
Bethsaida Luz- Sacred Dwelling of Light

Names

You called me *muñequita,*
Your sweet little doll, your *chiquitita.*

You called me *bruja,* but it was you
Who bewitched me, midnight to morning.

I surrendered my self to you,
Drifted in the breeze of your words.

You called me *vida,* to be yours always.
Our days together, unreined and sultry.

My heart beat like hummingbird wings.
My fine bones, entrusted to your safe keeping.

I became small, so small
I could fit in the palm of your hand.

Sometimes, I became so very small I could fit
In the thin dark space within your clenched fist.

And while I shrunk, you grew,
Doubled in dimension, mirrored in my eyes.

You delighted in your reflection, panicked if I blinked.
I kept my eyes open for your pleasure.

But my lids grew weary, my voice a whisper,
So soft you couldn't hear me.

There came a time I could barely hear my own voice,
Couldn't see my reflection through yours.

The day I ran away, you called me crazy—
Added me to your list of *locas*.

But now that my eyes have adjusted to the light, I see my name
Written on a roster of refugees.

Changing Horses Mid-Stream

I no longer like coffee
>so strong
>it leaves skid marks
>on my esophagus and explodes
>like a muddy racehorse at the finish line.

I no longer like guys
>so tough
>they aim to tame me,
>whip me into shape, bend me
>like Gumby's little sister.

Demure giggles of assent have been
>replaced with a robust WhatTheFuck?!

>>Sorry, the gal you're looking for isn't home.
>>Wait for her, you say?
>>Sorry, man. She ain't coming back.

Damage: A Love Story

Who hurt you? he asks,
     words bouncing off the pillow
     moist with sweat.
Not, Have you ever been hurt?
Just, Who hurt you?

A knot tightens in my neck, an answer
     seeps from the corners of my eyes
          further dampening the pillow
          beneath our brown curls.

I shift to keep my tears
     from trickling like a creek
          between tufted peaks
          of his chest.

He pours patience into the silence
     I hang between us.
I feel naked in a way that has nothing
     to do with our unclothed bodies
          entwined in rumpled sheets.

He occupies the space I failed to fill
     with his own bruised story.

I imagine his muscular frame
    fielding blows from a wife
      with wild eyes
    as he reveals
      that fractured year.

His question surrounds me
    like a mosquito net,
    buzzes like an insect
      I want to swat.

I have fought so hard
    to keep black and blue from oozing
      through now tough skin,
    keep labels like "victim"
    off my lapel.

Lavender and sage drift
    through an open window.
I exhale a wordless reply
    into the curve of his ear.

We shelter in a cocoon of arms and thighs,
    chest on chest, hearts hammering
      the door of the bulletproof safe
    ajar.

La Importancia de la Gramática y la Ortografía en el Amor

No confundas AMAR con AMARRAR.
No consiento ninguna jaula.
Necesito el aire fresco.
Soy pájaro de libre ala.

No confundas CASAR con CAZAR.
No significan lo mismo aunque solo
                    se le cambie una consonante.
No soy presa para capturar,
Me entrego libremente a mi amante.

No confundas que ser mi AMADO es lo mismo
                    que ser mi AMO.
No soy propiedad, ni esclava.
Nací libre y libre viviré
A tu lado, una igual, soberana y brava.

Punto.

Sunday Soundscape

Hum of a plane out of O A K.
Hip-hop playing high
      in a Chevy
      with the windows down.
A pit-bull barks.
A back door slams.

A teapot whistles and coffee trickles
      in the kitchen.
Keyboards clatter
      in the front room
      in tandem.
I feel the heat of you
      on my back.

Retinas soak in blue light,
      amplify appetites,
      deconstruct disasters.

You, a flood
      of info
      off the net.
Me, an avalanche
      of words
      on the page.

I slide thoughts
      from mind to screen
      but I'm sidetracked by your eyes
            gliding down my back.

With a click, you close Windows.
My click follows
      and computer drones
      disappear.

In the silence,
      the thrum of searching
      for each other
          crests
      like dolphins breaching waves

The Science of Pleasure

Your fingers trail down my spine
    like an *entitlement*.
You study me, know the caliber and curves
    of my wiring,
      styling with *science-based* certainty.

You disarm me
    with *diversity*
      in your moves,
    flood me with *evidence, based*
      in the sparkle of my synapses.

You transmute me, *trans*port me, en*gender*
    effervescence,
    eruption,
    leave me drifting
      on lava,
    vulnerable
      as a *fetus*
floating in its mama's womb.

Beauty's Cage

(after Ada Limón)

He doesn't care
        about wild hair
        mascara-smeared eyes
        sweat on skin

He gives no mind
        to my threadbare dress
        hands slide under, thrill
        bare thighs

It's me that enters
        beauty's cage, craves neat black lines
        around my eyes, curls that spiral
        in perfect place

When will I learn?
        he craves
        the bonbon
        not the wrapper

He/El

He lands unexpectedly,
lassos my time triumphantly.
I let go of the day, let him
lead the way,
lounge lazily.

Luscious licks and languid flicks
launch me, let me spiral and swirl,
unfurl a litany of glimmers,
make landfall,
heart like a lotus.

Treasure

You tease me
    with quick kisses,
    leave me wanting
        as you leap into the day
          like a cat—
    climbing fences, filling furrows,
    digging for bounty
    in overgrown yards.

You unearth mounds of poor man's prize:
    a gilded dish from a royal feast,
    fifteen feet of cotton twine,
    a 1950s swivel chair,
    plastic flowers for my hair.

You weave chartreuse quilts
    from prairie grass,
    live off waste of white man's way,
    find use for every screw and nail
    like your ancestors
        used every bit of skin and bone
          of bison that once roamed
            now-polluted plains.

Dusk is not enough
        to pause your toil—

You light the night with fireflies
        captured in a jar,
Build a bridge of Glow Sticks
        that towers towards the sky,
Scatter bits of albite
        to shimmer in the moon,
While I count the stars
        and wait
            for you
        to find your way
            back home.

Eastside Sidekick

By day you stashed your rescued ride
       down this lonely drive.
Came back to claim what's yours,
       me riding shotgun.

Warehouse and cottage sit side by side,
       sole sign of life the warm yellow light
           in the windows of a Painted Lady.

Clad in black, you blend with the night,
       mechanics' tools in one hand, machete in the other.

Chanting childhood rhymes,
       you tie up a muffler—

      Rock, paper, scissors...a machete slashes newsprint
           but can't match stone.

      Silent night, holy night, all is calm...'til it isn't.

Screech of rubber and a set of high beams
       wake me from sleep
           in the front seat of my car.

Midnight sentry turned canary
     in a tomcat's sights,
     my buggy gleams
        in the streetlight.

The intruder backs up and rolls away,
     but my pulse is pounding.

Sidekick in your thorny life,
I'm too familiar with these gritty streets.
I should be home by now, listening
     to the *rat-tat-tat* of the neighborhood,
        curled in a cozy quilt.

Unfiltered

Mid-sentence, you forbid me
Another sip,
Say I'll get dramatic, histrionic—
Words men love
For women's ire.

I lift my cup,
Let thick black brew
Slide down my throat.
So much down my throat.
Jammed
Down my throat.

Eyes locked like steel,
I take another swig,
Let it t
    r
     i
    c
     k
    l
     e
Luxuriously.

Coffee never tasted so good.

Hoisting Anchor

You sit in the first-mate seat picking indifference
        from between your teeth
While I navigate alone, squinting
        through a kaleidoscope to guide me.

Your silence wears thorns
        sharp as those on the cactus outside my window,
Cutting as cats' claws
        on the bare skin of my outstretched arm.

You tell me that you love me while I rub your belly, sated
        by the day,
Or when our mingled bodies
        spark.

You bring me glittering trinkets
        as midnight offerings,
Adorn me with sweet appellations,
        make me purr.

But I need more.

Love shouldn't mean being your ballast,
        making excuses for your absence
While you shuffle deck chairs

on the bow of a tilting ship.

In a calm sea of silence,
     swirls and starbursts give way
To a telescopic view
     of the shore.

A neon sun hangs low in the western sky.
All I can do is wish you well
And wave as our images undulate
     on widening water.

Pendulum

I put myself in your hands.
　　　You place possibility in my palms.
My fingers caress
　　　its contours,
　　　consider
　　whether to embed my fingerprints
　　　on what you offer.

You tell me the golden napkin ring is mine,
　　　yours, the black.

Your email arrives explaining you will:

　　　Send a text for short greetings.
　　　Email for something more complex.
　　　And sometimes ignore the rules
　　　when whimsy interjects.

Anything *I* should know? You ask.

　　　Maybe it's "the rules" that unsettle me
　　　　　as I slip
　　　　　into your ecosystem.

I feel like a feral cat that wandered
        through an open window,
        careful not to spill milk
        served in a silver bowl.

Your list makes mine look like scribbles
        on wine-stained napkins, like graffiti
        on cracked concrete walls.

What you should know is:

I'd never tag the cheeks of a Mona Lisa
        hanging in your living room.
But don't be surprised if you find a sonnet
        in red lipstick
        scrawled across your bedroom walls.

Rio

I need to change
       the tune circling
              the turntable.
Need to flip the disc
       from side A's love song
              to the B side ballad of friendship.

Spiraling wine and well-placed kisses,
       I believed
       I was Superwoman,
              able to soar.

Morning's bright sun revealed me
       more like Icarus,
       mere mortal, ill-equipped
              to fly
              or even swim.

We were rosewood arrows
       and morning glories
       at a muddy crossing.

I have no regrets.

But for now,

let cinders cool in blue water
Before we stumble again
across each other
In some small café with grass-cloth walls
along the river's edge.

Confection

My shrieks and giggles trail behind us.
Barefoot, draped across your lap,
  I hold on tight with every limb,
Sun glinting off the rim of your wheelchair
   as we careen down Durant Avenue.

You push sugar-spun hair out of silver eyes
   as we roll to a stop at an ice cream stand.
The apples of my cheeks are ripe.
"You two are delicious together!"
   says the pierced and tattooed twenty-something
   doling out cups and cones.

"You know, we're not a couple," you smile.

It doesn't matter that you once tried to tame me.
This love is too large for borders.

The Science of Tears

Scientists don't often cry
        so I was surprised to hear
        a quickly patched crack in his throat.

I sat across from him in Havana's heat,
        a summit to narrow the breach
        between our lands.

He delighted in his country's endeavors:
        diagnostic tools for developing nations,
        cures for cancer, novel vaccines.

But when he spoke of thwarted progress
        caused by the blockade,
        tears nearly betrayed him.

        Yet it was me who cried

        because misconceptions of Cuba are deeper and wider
            than 90 miles of sea,
        because the hearts that guide this rebel island
            are so damn fierce,
        because in that moment, I felt so much
            at home.

The scientist studied my tears and surrounded me in his arms.
He understood without a word.
Cuban scientists are smart that way.

Aviso

The day our eyes agreed
to slip off masks, you ask
when I first noticed you.
I say, you've always been
a butterfly fluttering
in the wings.

Your turn to confess,
you remember my smile
first bursting into your mind
in a place I've never been.

Poets fill space with pigment,
embellish with gold leaf,
count the beats in the breaths
between the lines.

We put our faith in moonlight,
believe in the hum of the earth
that only cats, *locos,* and bards
can hear.

You look to me as a mooring
to span the space between hearts.
But sometimes I am tremulous soil,

an unstable landing, known to turn
to quicksand under feet.

I am an unreliable narrator
in a poem with a nebulous arc.
I keep a lover in the closet,
serve moonshine
when it's time for tea.

When I say hearts were broken
and none of them were mine,
this is not brag, but warning.

I don't mean harm
but sometimes I leave
wounds
like a cat
with stiletto nails.

In the brown glow of your eyes,
I see warm honey
for tea and biscuits,
think this time could be different—
We have walked the same rough path to the sea,
both bow to the solstice like bookends.

But there is still the question of a landmass,
the lover in the closet, the risk it always is
to unsheathe one's heart.

The day our eyes agreed
to slip off masks, we heard
that tender thing with feathers
singing. But unlike birds and angels,
we don't have wings
and must tread gently.

Easter Tears

Easter Sunday
Dark
Aquarium corridors
Chattering children
Gaudy fish
Electric blue and neon pink
Dive and dart
Purple coral
Ocean greens
Sway on rippling currents
Brown-faced Groper
Floats like a zeppelin
Nuzzles thick plate glass
Searching
Sea urchin snacks
Children nibble
Chocolate bunnies and jellybeans
On our side of the divide
Brown-faced man
Sits on the floor
Before
Catfish
Crying
Tears
Streaming

Unseen
By passersby
The crowd swept by
Easter Sunday
Morning
He wept
In a darkened aquarium
Mourning
Once pure seas

Just Breathe

A solo scrub-jay perched on a wrinkled orange tree
        calls out dawn like nails
                on a chalkboard.

I can still remember mornings like symphonies
        and plump oranges
                on glossy green.

Oakland wakes to a gray brew
        of pollution and soot.
My sister can't stop coughing—
A wheeze planted its rusty roots in her
        once-pink lungs.

Pesticides drift,
        settle on a withered hibiscus.
Birds fall, bees die.

Monsanto—Not my saint!
Monsanto dances with the devil
        on a bed of crushed wings,
        dollars jingling in its pockets.

I recycle, reuse, reduce, but what can I do
        to curb corporate cravings

that shoot up towns and rainforests,
    greenhouse gases spurting
        from exit wounds.

Who would imagine we'd take to the streets and march
        for air to breathe
        for water to drink.

Thousands strong, our chants rising like ravens, we march
        for a future
        for this sacred Earth.

We march in the too-hot sun
        so sweet grass may always grow.

We march lest we leave our children
        a fractured sphere
and to our grandchildren, nothing
        but prayers.

All We Need is Love (and a New, Anti-Racist Praxis)

On the radio this morning, the Puerto Rican mother of a child
            slayed at Sandy Hook
        implored, in the name of her murdered daughter
            and her living Black son:

            Do not stop!
            Keep on marching!
            Do not stop short this time.

The world was splayed open
        Memorial Day eve
        by a nine-minute knee that broke
                the camel's back
                and George Floyd's windpipe,
        broke the other cheek
                we've been turning for centuries.

A weeping teen held her ground
                against blue mace,
        had no idea her Facebook post of a man
        moaning for his mama
                as a cop crushed his life
                        would reroute history.

The world paused on its axis—
        fire and throat,
        sacred rage and indignant love,
        hearts' prayers painted on boarded buildings.

Molecules trill
        beneath fifty million feet,
            path no longer immutable,
        gravity shifting
            with unity's weight.

Do not stop!

In the name of Breonna Taylor and Ahmaud Arbery,
        in the name of too many names to name,
        in the name of the never named...

Keep on marching!

'til we reach the corner of Justice and Main Streets,
        where every mother's child
            can breathe.

Do not stop short this time.

Love in the Time of COVID

Three days after the memo,
    how to shift from clinic to home,
    I realize these steps—
        undress in the doorway
        scrub in the shower
        sanitize cell phone
        and everything else
        we've touched—
    are meant to protect those we love.

Three days in, I laugh and relax
    homecoming rituals.

While my patients sleep in studio apartments
    six folks deep,
    my voice echoes in a thousand square feet,
    no one singing harmony.

I'm a potential vector, will not venture towards
    another warm body though I hunger
    to be held, to hear
        It's gonna be alright, Love,
    whispered in my ear.

I share pillow talk by telephone
　　with friends
　　　　holed up
　　　　in hellholes
　　　　of disease.

I have not touched another human for weeks—
　　aside from patients
　　　　whom I continue to see
　　with a two-way wave of caution,
　　　　each interaction
　　filled with compassion—
　　　　me for them and them for me.

A month ago, I thought nothing of helping someone
　　off an exam table.
Now, even this is a calculated risk.

As of last week, we are all masked—
　　I am learning how to smile
　　　　with just my eyes.

March 2020

Stuck in the Time of COVID

My muse must be in quarantine—
She isn't on the corner
  where she often thumbs a ride.
She's not among the wrinkled tarps
  where homeless folks reside.

The plaza's almost empty—
Masked men scrub the concrete clean.
Unmasked drivers chat between
  their daily ghost-bus runs.
Even the corner boys, selling remedies
  to make the boredom hum,
   are gone.

Then there's me—wrapped in a lab coat
   rescued from my closet's depth—
  padded shoulders make me look
   the superhero
   I'm supposed to be.

But I don't feel super—just sober,
   not hero, just over,
   just missing my muse.

I breathe in scents of fractured verse,
    can't grab them
    with my latex fists.
Shake shards of poems from folds
    in my mask, watch them melt
    in Purelled hands.

My refuge has been slumber—in bed at 8 p.m.
    patients' stories play in my mind again
    and again.

    Sandrita, just tortillas
        between her poking ribs.
    Marta, slicing paychecks
        to nourish those with less.
    Deirdre, desperate with desire,
        breaking all the rules.

¿Cómo estás? is filled with nuance.
¿ Cómo estoy? an existential flood.

I want to shelter-in-place, but an oath
    brings me back to work each day.
I want to serve, but I'm losing myself
    in a gap of uncertainty.
I seek sanctum of metaphor
    and imagery.

I scroll social feeds for my absent muse,
    hunt poems as salve
        for stress-stripped nerves,
    searching for the remedy
        I can't seem to find
  on sanitized clinic shelves.

April 2020

The Cobbler Has No Shoes
(for the late Dr. Lorna Breen)

How does it feel to blaze
      unmapped trails in bare feet,
      just a stethoscope
         as compass?

How do you bear the weight of being
      the final say, life or death in the balance—
         praying you get it right.

      Hands you cannot hold
         grasp at life.
      Fierce coughs,
         fevered delirium.
         No way to turn off
            the volume.

      Placing breathing tubes in the morning,
         toe tags at night.
      Some nightmares don't dispel
         at dawn.

What thought screamed before
    scalpel sliced skin with precision
        gleaned from years
           of cutting
              out a body's ills?

What final thought before crimson
    flowed
        across
           white
              sheets?

Who was there to hold and heal
    the healer?

Who placed the toe tag
    on the doctor's unshod feet?

April 2020

Grounded
(after Lucille Clifton)

Here, between starshine and soil,
      I lay myself before you.
You, raven gliding high overhead, see me
      sit atop a ridge of clay,
      watch the bay glisten below.

For ten months I've been confined
to ten square blocks, take the same walk
      day after day...after day.
For ten months, I've watched the Oakland airport
      from this ridge,
planes once spouting into the sky
      like a geyser,
      now just a trickle.

I once rode those planes
      to dizzying places.
Now, I am grounded, naked
      feet in moist soil,
the atoms and molecules that I am,
      contained within
      the boundaries of my skin,
the stardust and spirit that I am,
      untethered.

January 2021

The Night That Lupe Died
(in memory of Guadalupe Elizondo)

The wind howled something awful—
tossed garbage cans and give-away boxes
filled with things we no longer need.

We learn we don't need much at all,
find blessings in the rise and fall of our chests,
the taste of sugar on our tongues.

The wind wailed, banged garden gates, flung cast-off
clothing into the street, pounded fists on the heavens
like a daughter whose mother has died in her arms.

We taste the salt
of her wounds.
Suck air through our teeth.

The night that Lupe died, the answers to questions
we'd yet to ask were lost in the wind.
The key to her diary slipped into a crevice.

Trees thrashed a charcoal night.
Soon, the sky will crack
and rain will rage

for forty days
as it rained for Noah when
the world was too damaged to endure.

Rain will mold our houses,
mottle our skin,
puff our eyes.

But one day, the mist will lift,
a dove will land, and a glimmer
we never noticed will appear

in an indigo sky, shine on a girl dancing
in moonlight, her toes tracing lines
her mother once carved in their garden,

a silver key on a red ribbon
dangling from a branch
of a banyan tree.

Black Sandals

Footbed now frayed at the front edge,
    a pair of sandals found in winter
    on the clearance rack at Ross,
    "out-of-season" merchandise
        perfect for my plans.

Feet strapped to cushioned soles,
I was ready to roam—
        could nearly smell the loam of El Yunque,
        feel the Caribbean kissing
        my bare toes, footwear dangling
            from fingertips.

I was ready to melt in embraces cautiously
        stored like last year's Christmas ornaments,
        to hear the giggles of grandnieces
        now a head taller, quizzically
        trying to recall
            who I am.

But instead, my plans hit a halt like an em-dash.

My sandals walk
        the ups and downs
        of my neighborhood, stroll

past stucco facades of California bungalows,
            new boundaries of my sphere.

This pandemic year has worn my soles.
I walk in circles
        alone,
            clutching blessings.

Today, sunshine cracks the blinds,
            news inoculates my daydreams—

I inhale wild orchids twining a hilltop
            in Guaynabo.
Sit across a table from Tanama and ask,
            ¿Cómo estás querida?
Cry at Titi Sara's grave.
Dry my feet, damp with sea in Luquillo.

I will wear out whatever life is left
            in the soles of these shoes.
I will dare to plan again,
            fragile as that may be.

April 2021

I Turn to Prayer

There are no atheists in foxholes
~ (source uncertain)

On a planet where the sun rises red
and the moon glows amber
    like a spoon of honey
    in a coffee sky, a virus still rages
      like the fires
    flaming five million acres
    of forests and homes.

Good and bad hair days
    have been replaced by
good and bad air days—
And for a heap of weeks,
    our air has been a mess.

I mask for ash-filled skies and COVID
all rolled into an apocalyptic brew
    in a nation debating masks
      all the way to the grave yard.

Now, pestilence snakes
    through the White House halls—
Trump got the bug, karmic justice

and just plain disdain
finally catching up with him.

I'm not one to wish folks ill,
         though the man throws kindling
              on wildfires
              of injustice.
I don't want to be crass, so
         I turn to prayer—

May the flame of COVID's fever burn
         white supremacy from his brain.
May walking death's highway teach him
         how much life matters—
              black & brown lives too.

October 2020

Orange

I once loved orange, the color
        of my mother's mohair sweater
                and my father's flannel shirt.
        Snuggled between them, scent
                of wool and autumn leaves,
                we wandered Berkshire days.

I once loved the fiery orange sun that sunk
        on a pink feather bed over Long Island Sound,
                seagulls gliding above.

I once loved sweet *chinas,* juice dripping orange
        down my wrists as I peeled their thick skin
                in the back seat of a rickety Jeep,
                engine straining
        as we climbed Puerto Rico's *cordillera* into the clouds,
                fertile orange earth
                        peeking between green.

Orange was once sacred—
        like the robes of Buddhist monks,
        like a pinch of saffron in Persian stews,
        like *achiote,* coloring a *caldero* of *arroz*
                steaming on the stove
                while Danny Rivera croons
                        on the radio.

You have taken orange and turned it into an atrocity.
Your version of orange is
        a flashing neon sign in Vegas
             where you gambled
             with our lives
        sporting an overdone tan
             of the idle rich.

I've long been wary of ruddy-faced men,
imagine the red of their cheeks not fine arteries
        beneath pale skin, but a mirror
            reflecting blood
            shed by their hands
      or by their ancestors
              who hand down their loot.

You moved Monopoly pieces on a tilted board,
             amassed hotels
        while swelling numbers of people sleep
            in the street
      and others break their backs and their children's
            piggy banks
      to pay Bank of America.

You damaged decency,
poured gasoline on simmering bigotry
            and lit it
        with an orange match.

Keep your damn orange—
    the orange stink of a polluted pond,
        eco-friendly laws tossed
           in your dumpster,
    the orange air when the sun couldn't shine
        through fire ash,
    the orange rust that accumulates on a heart
        whose owner has forgotten
           how to use it.

I take back my orange—
    apricot and peach
        hanging heavy on leafy limbs,
    the cantaloupe walls
        of my kitchen,
    the soft glow of dawn.

Aquí Se Habla Español

Mimi told me
        her tongue was whipped
        by a wasp of a woman
            for speaking
                Spanish.

This was not rural Florida, a Burger King
        where days before
      two white patrons pounced
      the Puerto Rican manager,
      told him to go back to his "Mexican country"
        for speaking
            Spanish.

This was liberal San Francisco, the Presidio,
        former fortress by the sea
            seized by the U.S. from Mexico
                in a bloody land-grab war.

I might've flicked the wasp away, snarled
      "Translate this!!"
           middle finger in the air.
But Mimi wears pearl earrings and said,
      "Excuse me?!"
           right eyebrow hiked to her hairline.

What's happening to the Bay?
Who's flipping *barrios* to bohemian chic?
Who's arrived?
What do they add and subtract?
And who does the math?

Money pours in through silicon
        while black and brown stream out.

Realtors are the new rock stars.
        Mortgage bankers rumble the bass.
                And they're all gettin' high
                    on the boom.

We said goodbye to a neighbor
        off to convert
                gritty factories
                        to glittery condos.

A pin-striped party guest asked, "Where?"
"Jingletown," she giggled.

I leaned in with Oakland history of that
        working-class Mexican neighborhood—
How back in the day, men coming home could be heard
        half a block away,
                day's pay
                    jingling
                        in their pockets.

My story was sliced midair by the pin-striped guest—
    "Is it safe??"
I'd said Mexican. He'd heard Criminal.

I left the bash, shared my despair with a friend.

        "He may not be the racist you say," he said,
           playing devil's advocate.

        (Who the hell lawyers for Lucifer?!)

        "People get a certain image
           when you say ghetto," he added.

        "I didn't say 'ghetto'—
          I said 'working-class Mexican neighborhood.'"

¡Dios mío! ¡Ayúdanos Señor!

        ****

In the locker room at a public pool,
    two English speakers ping-pong words.
Consonants bounce
    off concrete walls,
    sprout an ache
        in the nape of my neck.
    I hold my tongue—they have every right.

But when I think of Mimi,
      of who's allowed, who's disavowed,
          bile burns my mouth.

I summon antidotes, distill words,
          conjure
          what Mimi might've said:

    Esta linda tierra era mexicana.
    Todavía se oyen los dulces retumbos.
    Aquí, <u>sí</u>, se habla español.

On a Mission
(homage to La Lunada Literary Lounge & San Francisco's Mission District)

I balance on metal teeth of a rising stairway,
       slow motion serenade,
              cellos echo
                     in a train station's cavern.

The teeth tuck themselves behind a concrete lip,
       spit me into a plaza of *papel picado*
              filled with fruits and flowers
              and a preacher
              screeching "*en el nombre de Dios.*"

A packed McDonald's holds down one corner,
Taquería San José secures another.

Men with calloused hands eat
       foods spiced with richness of their roots
       on tables topped with oilcloth
              in bare bulb *luz*
       while the gentry devour the neighborhood
              by candlelight
              on white linen.

But I am not here to eat—

I came to follow the moon
        as it scurries up lamp posts,
                runs along phone lines,
                        alights on a cloud like an eagle
                                with a snake in its mouth.

I follow the serpent, slither down 24th street
        under a blue moon, super moon, blood moon
                eclipsed by the sun.

I pass Burbujas Lavandería where overworked mothers
        wash clothes dragged down
                from overfilled flats
        while their children draw dreams
                on cracked sidewalks.

Mission musicians in a multi-hued mural, crown
        the parking lot of House of Brakes.
        Low-riders fist-bump with a nod.

I finally arrive at my Mecca
        early.
This is the only place in my life I arrive
        early.

I gaze at rows of chairs
        through diamond shapes of a security gate,

can almost taste the pregnant air,
>
> like a snake, a *bruja*, a poet with words
> on my tongue.

The doors fly open and I flow in like water
> to a low spot, though I'm on a high.

I'm all adrenalin and dragonflies
> and those sparks that leap between synapses.

I sit beside home-girls who pump poems
> out of fire hydrants, spray stories
> that hang in the air like gossamer.

Brothers born and raised in this *barrio* bounce words
> behind their backs, dribble and pass,
> shoot a three-pointer, slam dunk their verse.

A sister sings her truth and rings rafters
> and those tender places that we hide inside,
> *tú sabes...*

Walking back to BART in the dark,
> the neighborhood's in a different mood.
The bookstores and fruit stands are tucked in
> for the night.
Guys with tight jeans and gaudy voices spill
> out of corner bars.

The fluorescent light and *ranchera* music
    flowing from Taquería Vallarta
        is pumped up
    like it's wearing 6-inch heels.

But I am wearing sensible shoes and the full moon
    illuminates my steps.
I spout poetry to myself like a lunatic,
    figure no one's gonna bother a *loca*
        walking alone in the night.

McDonald's is still open. A man in just a loincloth,
    yellow flowers in his matted hair,
        steps into the chilly air,
          a red heart
          painted on his chest.

Maybe he's a *loco de verdad.*
Or maybe he's just like me, in camouflage.

Eyes meet, we exchange a "Good Night,"
    and I descend into the cavernous station.

    Mission accomplished.

Through the Alley

Behind gray fence and tree now bare
From paper bag a hurried meal
He doesn't know I see him there

Snowflakes float on frosted air
His collar up against the cold
Behind gray fence and tree now bare

Fingers stiff, no gloves to wear
He rubs and blows to keep them warm
He doesn't know I see him there

Hat pulled over matted hair
No place to bathe, to dress, to groom
Behind gray fence and tree now bare

Come night he makes himself a lair
Of arrow wood and bramble weed
He doesn't know I see him there

With morning and the bright sun's glare
His homelessness he hides away
Behind gray fence and tree now bare
He doesn't know I see him there

Sparks

Brother poet teaches me
  how to catch fireflies,
  those glimmering sparks
    that flicker in my mind.

He tells me: pull over when a muse trails you
    in the fast lane—
  No way you wanna mess with a muse.

But there's no soft shoulder to pull over
  on San Leandro Boulevard—
Just a high curb holding a river of weeds, graffiti,
  and makeshift shelters multiplying
    faster than the thistles and thorns.
There's nothing soft about my route
  through East Oakland.

I park in the employee lot and cross the street
  dodging red light runners and rats
    that leap like pole vaulters into air vents.

I'm late for work
  but a muse caught a ride on my tail pipe,
  held me in her silky hands, pinned my eyelids
    open wide.

My gaze traces the corrugated bark of a palm tree
        towering above the Fruitvale BART.

Not fifty feet away, Oscar Grant got shot
        dead
        by a cop who said
                he'd confused right from left
                but really confused right from wrong
                        as he pulled his gun
                                on a handcuffed man
                                face down
                                on the platform.
I'm late for work
        but palm frond shadows
                dance on the pavestones
        and women who walked all the way
        from Guatemala
                rest
                in the shade
                wearing handwoven huipils
                and high heeled shoes from PayLess.

Girls with black braids
        skip 'round the fountain,
        clap hands in blue water,
                giggle their delight.

I scribble snapshots in my calendar,

in the leftover corners of days.
I might as well be the palm tree, the fountain,
the aroma of coffee
in the plaza.

I'm late for work
but the sun spells summer
on my shoulders,
brother poet's voice
is in my ears,
and there are fireflies everywhere
I look.

notes

on "Borinquen"

Borinquen—(or Borikén), is the name the indigenous Taino people gave to their island home now known as Puerto Rico. The name has changed over the years as imposed by various colonial powers. Spain controlled the island from 1493 to 1898. It was then claimed by the U.S. as bounty after the Spanish-American War (despite Spain having granted self-governance to the island in the previous year.)

Commentary on the $72 Billion Debt—It would take many pages to explain the history of the approximate $72 billion debt which Puerto Rico defaulted on in 2016, but suffice it to say the debt is the result of colonialism, tax-free profit-taking, financial manipulations and graft. The U.S. has not allowed Puerto Rico to declare bankruptcy on this debt. Instead, they established PROMESA, a U.S.-controlled fiscal board charged with restructuring the debt. The result has been severe austerity measures imposed on the populace. Nearly 300 schools and numerous other community institutions have been closed. Wages, university budgets, and already meager pensions have been cut. Public lands and operation of utilities have been privatized. In other words, they are paying off investors at the expense of the island's basic services and wellbeing of the people ("they dare to tell you, it's your own damn fault").

Since writing this poem in 2016, there has been significant protest over the debt.The chant heard on the streets is: *Esa deuda es illegal, y no lo vamos a pagar* (That debt that has been imposed on us is illegal and we are not going to pay it). Canceling the debt is a crucial issue for the island.

Querido Caribe—was written just after Hurricane Irma rammed the Caribbean. Puerto Rico was hit, but not badly, and opened its doors to hurricane refugees from the Virgin Islands where Irma had caused heavier damage. ("help comes from those with bare shelves sharing their pot of rice"). Cuba was also hit by Irma. In that same week, I received an email from my artist friend Crispin Sarra in Havana, containing an image of a painting he had just completed of a giant rooster titled: *Gallo para Amigos* (Rooster for Friends). This poem was inspired by the love and neighborly aid demonstrated across the Caribbean in the face of natural disaster, while the U.S. government sorely lagged in providing relief.

María—On Sept. 20, 2017, Hurricane María devastated Puerto Rico with torrential rains and 155 mph winds. The island was nearly incommunicado with transmission towers having been knocked down. This poem takes place a few days after the storm, at a *Bombazo*, a gathering where musicians and dancers interact in an Afro-Taino tradition known as *Bomba*. The drums used in *Bomba* are referred to as *barriles,* meaning barrels, because this was what the drums were originally made from. *Cuembe* is the name of one of the traditional *Bomba* rhythms. A *cuembe* is usually upbeat and flowy, its rhythm described like waves of the ocean. But that day, the room was filled with angst as we waited to hear from friends and family on the island—thus the mournful tone of the *cuembe*.

Poeta en San Juan—This poem is based on a story told to me by my step-grandson Andrés, who weathered Hurricane María in San Juan. Of note, *Plena* is a music and dance form that emerged from Puerto Rico's African roots. The rhythm is played on flat, handheld drums called *panderos*. The songs of *Plena* were often called the people's newspaper because this is how news was disseminated.

Ode to Tití—Sara Morales was my beloved aunt by marriage. Tití was one of approximately 4,000 people who died on the island in the aftermath of Hurricane María primarily due to lack of food, clean water, electricity, and medical attention. Even before the hurricane, Puerto Rico's infrastructure was shaky due to a decade-long recession and poor management of an aging electrical system. The combination of devastatingly high winds and a power grid in disrepair resulted in a complete loss of electricity (with some areas waiting 18 months before electricity was restored). Without power, water could not be pumped, food spoiled without refrigeration, and medical devices were inoperable. These conditions contributed to the death toll.

Return: Against the Flow—1) Note on translation: In Spanish, *afuera* literally means "outside," not "away," but it is a term some people in Puerto Rico use to indicate the world beyond Puerto Rico. The old man wanted to move away from the island, go *afuera*.

2) *Preciosa* is the name of a song written by Rafael Hernández in 1937. Its beautiful lyrics express a deep love for Puerto Rico. *Preciosa* is considered an unofficial National Anthem of the island.

Better Homes & Gardens: Puerto Rico Edition— "vultures flying circles in the sky" refers to the vulture capitalists that descended on Puerto Rico after Hurricane María—investors trying to make a financial killing by taking advantage of intensified vulnerabilities and economic hardship including rampant foreclosures resulting from the storm.

Castles in the Air—This particular house is located in Santurce, behind the Hilton hotel. As the story was told to me, the hotel wanted to buy and bulldoze the house to expand their parking lot.

Cleaning House—Puerto Rico's Governor Ricardo "Ricky" Roselló announced his resignation on July 24, 2019, following two weeks of daily marches that grew like wildfire. On July 17 alone, more than half a million people took to the streets of Old San Juan in protest. Given that the island has only about three million residents, that is a hugely impressive number. The protests were sparked by the public revelation of a private group chat between Roselló and his staff which included vulgar, sexist, misogynistic, homophobic, and racist language. Roselló also pointedly mocked people, including those who had died due to Hurricane María. Boricuas poured into the streets with their *panderos, barriles de bomba*, and pots to bang, the message undeniable—*¡Basta ya! ¡Ricky renuncia!* (Enough already! Rick, resign!)

Cartography of the Caribbean—Suni Cabrera lived across the hall from Tití Sara in an apartment building overlooking Laguna San José in Carolina, Puerto Rico. That is how we met and became fast friends. Among the many things Suni collects are maps. She showed me copies of maps drawn in the early 1500s showing Puerto Rico as the center of everything. Modern-day map makers have charted the world differently, with Puerto Rico appearing as just a speck on the globe. But those who know and love Borinquen know that those early mapmakers had actually gotten it right.

on "Afuera"

As mentioned earlier, in Spanish, *afuera* means "outside," but it is a term some people use in Puerto Rico to indicate the world outside the island. I use it here in that spirit.

Song of Refuge—I originally wrote this poem with the DACA youth in mind. But I extend this poem to all people, anywhere, in need of safety and shelter.

Something from Nothing—Written in memory of my uncle Sam Weiner who worked as an optician in the polyglot neighborhood of Flushing, Queens, NY. Uncle Sammy took pride in always saying "hello" and "goodbye" in the language of everyone he met.

Sancocho—Written in a workshop led by Martín Espada and inspired by the poem he presented: Nicolás Guillén's "My Last Name."

Behind the Eight Ball—This is a persona poem (I don't usually get into pool hall brawls.)

La Importancia de la Gramática y la Ortografía en el Amor—The title translates to: "The Importance of Grammar and Spelling in Love". No English translation of the poem is provided here because I contend the poem is not translatable. (If you, dear reader, can prove me wrong and translate the poem into

English, I will send a free, signed copy of this book to the first person to successfully do so.)

The Science of Pleasure—The "CDC Poetry Project" was started by art-activists who encouraged poets to write poems incorporating the seven words the Trump administration forbade the CDC (Center for Disease Control) to use: *entitlement, science-based, diversity, evidence-based, transgender, vulnerable, and fetus.* This poem was my submission to the project.

Rio—Back in the day, we listened to music on vinyl discs that we'd spin on turntables. The small "45s" had a song on each side, an A side and a B side song.

The Science of Tears—The U.S. has maintained an economic blockade against Cuba since 1960. It is the longest lasting trade embargo in modern history and has contributed to economic adversities on the island.

Just Breathe—Written on Sept. 8, 2018, the day of the *Rise for Climate, Jobs and Justice* march in San Francisco.

Love in the Time of COVID—I have been working as a Physician Assistant at *La Clinica de la Raza* in Oakland, California since 1980. I had planned to retire at the start of 2020, but when COVID hit, I decided to stay on to help support our community which ended up being hit disproportionately hard. This was the first of a series of COVID poems I wrote (all dated at bottom of the page to trace the chronology of the pandemic).

The Cobbler Has No Shoes—Dr. Lorna Breen was the Medical Director at the New York Presbyterian Hospital in Manhattan. In that role, she was on the frontlines of the early battle against COVID. She herself fell ill with COVID. Subsequently, exhausted and working long shifts to try to save lives while the death count mounted, she apparently reached the limit on what she could bear. Dr. Breen took her own life on April, 26, 2020.

The Night That Lupe Died—Guadalupe Elizondo was a dear friend, neighbor, and Stanford-trained Physician Assistant. We worked together at *La Clínica* in Oakland taking care of our community for 40 years. Lupe was extraordinarily generous in so many ways and dealt with life's challenges with grace and determination. She delighted in being a mother and adored Alejandra, her beloved daughter. Lupe died unexpectedly while visiting family in Mexico this past January. She was so loved and is so missed. I wrote this poem as a reflection on grief and as a prayer for Alejandra.

Orange—This poem was written in a workshop led by Martín Espada. The prompt was to write about someone or something you truly despise. This was my response and my contribution to the process of "decolonizing the color orange".

On a Mission—When I first started writing and reading my poetry aloud, I would faithfully trudge off to La Lunada Literary Lounge held at La Galería de la Raza on 24th St. in SF's Mission

District held each month under the full moon. It was there that I cut my teeth as a poet. I am forever grateful to Sandra García Rivera (my poetic *madrina* who first christened me "Poet"), who curated the wonderful space where so many of us emerged as writers and congealed as a community.

Sparks—I had been composing this poem in my head for weeks—every morning on my way to work. But it would vanish from my memory by the time I'd get home each evening. At the urging of my brother-poet norm mattox, one day I stopped and wrote it down. I dedicate this poem to norm.

❧

classroom guide

Theme: **COLONIALISM**

Colonialism is an act of economic and political domination involving the control of a country and its people by an external power. In most cases, the goal of colonizers is to profit by exploiting the resources of the countries they dominate.

Prompts:

- **What are the characteristics of a colonial relationship between nations?**

- **What nations and territories are currently under colonial rule, and by which countries?**

- **The U.S., which was established by the American War of Independence from Britain's colonial rule, currently has colonies of its own (Puerto Rico being one of them). Discuss this dichotomy.**

Representative poems that embody the history of colonial exploitation of Puerto Rico include:

      o "Commentary on the $72 Billion Debt"
      o "Cartography of the Caribbean"

Theme: **HURRICANE MARÍA & HOW WE PROCESS NEWS**

Hurricane María devastated Puerto Rico in September 2017. Somewhere around 4,000 people died in the aftermath. News stories that report disasters of this magnitude can overwhelm the viewer with their enormity. The poet uses stories of particular people and houses to awaken understanding and empathy for those affected by the disaster.

Prompts:

- **How do you view the role of poetry as an educational tool or a way to disseminate information?**

- **Describe how these poems, written about historical occurrences and recent news**

events, make you feel? How do they influence your thinking? How might they influence your actions?

- **Were there any poems, stanzas, or lines that particularly stood out to you? If so, which ones and in what way?**

Representative poems:
- o "María"
- o "Castles in the Air"
- o "Water View House for Sale"
- o "Return Against the Flow"

Theme: THE ROLE OF POETRY in EDUCATION and in SELF-EXPRESSION

Poetry encourages us to think "outside the box", shows us that there can be different interpretations of a poem (or situation). It stimulates our ability to conceptualize and encourages us to cultivate our own understanding of things. By appealing to the emotional parts of our brain, poetry can help us learn through empathy. By writing, we sometimes come to understand our own feelings and find ways to express them to others.

Prompts:

- **Does a poem such as "Unaccompanied Minors," which describes the effect of immigration policies on an individual person, prompt more empathy in contrast to news stories that speak in generalities? Why or why not?**

- **Do any of the poems in this section inspire you to write your own poem on self-identity, social justice, or love? (If so, please write!)**

    and/or

- **Write a poem using any of the following "stems" (line starts). Feel free to use more than one of these stems in your poems.**
    - o "There was no time to wait..."
    - o "Our kitchen steamed aromas..."
    - o "A fading photo lets me know..."
    - o "Your fingers trail down my spine..."
    - o "Morning's sun revealed..."
    - o "Soon, the sky will crack..."
    - o "My story was sliced..."
    - o "It sounds like old news when..."

o "We sang the chorus..."
o "A suitcase and a one-way ticket..."
o "Where will you go..."

Main themes and representative poems:

Immigration, xenophobia, and the struggle to belong
o "Unaccompanied Minors..."
o "Song of Refuge"
o "How Does a Four-Year-Old Know"

Love
o "Treasure"
o "Confection"
o "Damage: A Love Story"

Break-ups
o "Names"
o "Hoisting Anchor"
o "Rio"

Racism
o "All We Need Is Love (and a New Anti-Racist Praxis)"
o "Nightmares"
o "Mistaken Identity: Facebook Pegged Me Wrong"

acknowledgments

Many thanks to J. K. Fowler and Nomadic Press for selecting my manuscript for publication. Michaela Mullin—I could not have dreamed of a better editor! Thank you for your gentle style and for sharing my belief that laughter and serious literature can co-exist.

To Luís Pérez, who painted the beautiful mural that appears on the cover of this book (and to Yano Rivera for locating him in Puerto Rico!)

To all the "Querid@s Compañer@s" from La Tertulia Boricua for being such a warm and supportive community with whom I first shared my poetry, paper trembling in my hands and all.

To Piri Thomas *(en paz descanse)* who inspired Silvia Torres and me to create La Tertulia Boricua in 2011.

To all my teachers and mentors, with special thanks to Sharon Coleman and the poetry program at Berkeley City College.

To all the Open Mic hosts who elevate poetry and make space for those of us who love to write and listen.

To Daniel Rudman, dear friend, writer, actor, and director, who taught me how to make poems come alive, not only on the page but also on the stage.

To my family for your love, for being proud of me, and for cheering me on.

To all the writers and friends who have been so supportive in so many ways, who have become like siblings and cousins. If I try to list you all, I know I will inadvertently leave someone out, so I won't. But you know who you are, and hopefully, know how much I appreciate you!

Thank you for walking this journey with me.

I extend my appreciation to the following presses and anthologies for first publishing the following poems from this collection, some in earlier versions.

About Place Journal *The Cobbler has No Shoes, Sparks;* **Borderlands: Texas Poetry Review** *Unaccompanied Minors, Aquí Se Habla Español;* **Civil Liberties United** (anthology) *No, I'm Not the Maid and Other Micro-aggressions;* **Culture Counts Magazine** *Love in the Time of COVID, Stuck in the Time of COVID;* **Home** (anthology) *Song of Refuge;* **La Respuesta** *Behind the Eight Ball;* **MeowMeowPowPow Press** *Poeta en San Juan;* **Moonstone Arts Center** *All We Need is Love (and a New, Anti-Racist Praxis);* **Nueva York Poetry Review** *Decolonize Your Mind, La Importancia de la Gramática y la Ortografía en el*

Amor; **Poets Reading the News** *Cartography of the Caribbean, I Turn to Prayer, Orange;* **Shanti Arts: Still Point Arts Quarterly** *Just Breathe;* **The Acentos Review** *María, Querido Caribe (English and Spanish);* **Toho Journal** *How to Keep Cool When a Hurricane Knocks Out the Power,* **The Pencil Dreams** (anthology) *Ode to Titi, Confection;* **Writing for Peace: DoveTales** *Cleaning House, Castles in the Air, Nightmares, Mistaken Identity*

SUSANA PRAVER-PÉREZ

Susana Praver-Pérez is a Pushcart-nominated poet and a winner of the San Francisco Foundation / Nomadic Press Literary Prize for Poetry (2021). Born and raised in New York, Susana currently resides in Oakland, California, where she works as a Physician Assistant at La Clínica de la Raza.

Susana has studied Creative Writing at: Naropa Institute's Summer Poetics program, U.C. Berkeley's Poetry for the People, at countless workshops including Las Dos Brujas, and at Berkeley City College from which she holds a Certificate in Creative Writing/Poetry.

Susana's poems have appeared in numerous literary journals and anthologies.

Hurricanes, Love Affairs, & Other Disasters is her first full-length book of poetry.

OTHER WAYS TO SUPPORT NOMADIC PRESS' WRITERS

In 2020, two funds geared specifically toward supporting our writers were created: the **Nomadic Press Black Writers Fund** and the **Nomadic Press Emergency Fund.**

The former is a forever fund that puts money directly into the pockets of our Black writers. The latter provides up to $200 dignity-centered emergency grants to any of our writers in need.

Please consider supporting these funds. You can also more generally support Nomadic Press by donating to our general fund via nomadicpress.org/donate and by continuing to buy our books. As always, thank you for your support!

Scan here for more information and/or to donate. You can also donate at nomadicpress.org/store.